Published by: Boulder Press, P.O. Box 1583, Solana Beach, Ca 92075

Photography and Text © 2013 Mike Barton. Photographer's website: www.mikebartonphoto.com

Individual prints may be purchased directly from the photographer: cell phone 720 934-4322

No part of this book may be reproduced in any form without written permission from the publisher.

Editor: David L. Miles, Co-director Harsha House Museum, Charlevoix (Michigan) Historical Society

Library of Congress Control Number: 2012923033

ISBN 13: 978-0-9801024-3-7
ISBN 10: 0-9801024-3-X
First Printing: 2013
Printed in China

SOLVANG

photography and text by Mike Barton
foreword by Olympic Gold Medalist Todd Rogers

BOULDER PRESS

Contents

5	Foreword	65	Doors and Windows
7	Introduction	81	Danish Gardens
23	The Village	89	A Look Inside
43	Windmills and Towers	95	Around the Valley
51	Festivals and Celebrations	109	About the Photographer

SOLVANG

Foreword

If you are looking for the glitz and neon lights of the big city, you won't find it here in Solvang. However, if you are looking for a beautiful sunset walk followed by a great glass of vino, you've found your spot.

Solvang sits up on a plateau overlooked on one side by the coastal mountains and the Los Padres National Forest on the other side. It is less than ten miles to the Pacific Ocean as the crow flies and has mostly a mild climate due to the proximity of the ocean and the marine influence.

I moved to Solvang so my family and I could fully enjoy the quality of life Solvang has to offer. It is a beautiful little city originally founded by Danish settlers a little over one hundred years ago.

When I first walked through Solvang I felt comfortable and at home with the all the windmill buildings and bakeries cooking up the delicious Danish dessert, abelskivers. Now when I walk through Solvang, I find myself saying hello and waving my hand to half the people I pass. That is just the kind of place it is.

There is a sense of peace and tranquility that permeates life in Solvang. That fits my personality and the way I like to live my life away from the volleyball court.

There is a focus on family, specifically on the kids in our community, that I have not found anywhere else. When I moved here I had two very young children and in the ten years we have been here, I have never once regretted the move for me or my family.

Todd Rogers, who teamed with Phil Dalhausser, won the Olympic gold medal in men's beach volleyball at the 2008 Summer Olympics in Beijing. Todd grew up in nearby Santa Barbara and graduated from University of California, Santa Barbara. Rogers and his family moved to Solvang in 2002 because of the slower pace of life.

Rasmussens is a Solvang landmark specializing in gifts from Europe and Scandinavia.

Introduction

Velkommen til Solvang, a charming little village nestled in California's Santa Ynez Valley. Founded in 1911 by three Danish-American educators, Solvang (Danish for "sunny fields"), has the feel of northern Europe due to the Danish-style architecture, authentic Scandinavian bakeries and the many windmills that seem to be around every corner. It's no wonder it's known as California's "Little Denmark."

Located just 125 north of Los Angeles, Solvang's Scandinavian tradition, colorful buildings, flower-lined streets dotted with stores, cafes, galleries, pastry shops, toy stores, wine-tasting rooms and other establishments draw visitors from all over the world. The downtown is very compact, making it easy to explore on foot.

Since Solvang is surrounded by the vineyards of the Santa Ynez Valley wine country, it's easy to tour some of the more than 80 nearby wineries. You can also visit an ostrich farm, nearby horse ranches or a lavender farm.

The Santa Ynez Valley was originally inhabited by the Chumash Indians. Spanish missionaries arrived in the early 19th century and founded the Old Mission Santa Inés in 1804 in Solvang.

LEFT: In the fall, you will find this pumpkin patch along Alamo Pintado Road near Solvang.

OPPOSITE PAGE CLOCKWISE: Decisions, decisions at Olsen's Danish Village Bakery. Participants in the annual 35 and 50-mile Solvang Prelude cycling event ride through the village and turn up Atterdag Road as the early morning fog begins to lift. A four-wheel surrey with a fringed top passes by the Visitors Center.

In the mid 1800s, ranchers and farmers began to settle in the Santa Ynez Valley. Initially, the stagecoach was the popular way to travel in and out of the valley. The narrow-gauge railroad provided a more convenient means of transportation and serviced the valley from 1887 to 1934.

Beginning in 1850, a great number of Danes immigrated to the United States due to poor economic conditions and established many Danish communities around the country but not in California. Benedict Nordentoft was an educator and clergyman born in Denmark. He traveled to the United States in 1898 to help coordinate relations between Danish Lutheran churches scattered around the Midwest and East Coast. Nordentoft, along with Jens. M. Gregersen and Peder P. Hornsyld, came up with the idea of creating a Danish colony in California and formed the Danish-American Colony Company in San Francisco.

In 1911, the group bought almost 9,000 acres in the Santa Ynez Valley and about 40 Danish-Americans settled there by the end of the year. It quickly became apparent that the remaining plots of land were not selling and this put a strain on the company's finances. Gregersen traveled to Danish colonies in the Midwest and convinced many immigrants to buy plots in Solvang.

Nordentoft was not happy with the town's tiny folk school, located where the Bit O'Denmark Restaurant is today, so he established Atterdag College in 1914. The larger facility sat on a hilltop above the village and served the community until it was torn down in 1970.

Many Danes turned to farming and became quite successful. Others focused on building a town, and before long Solvang had a hotel, a general store, blacksmith shop, barbershop, a bank, a lumberyard, an auto garage and a post office.

With the exception of the Bethania Evangelical Lutheran Church (1928) that resembles rural churches in Denmark, the early architectural style of Solvang did not have the Danish look until the 1940s.

Annual Danish-style celebrations include A Taste

INTRODUCTION

of Solvang, Danish Days and Julefest. Solvang is also a popular destination for cyclists, and has hosted the annual Tour of California, a professional cycling stage race. The 2004 Oscar-winning film "Sideways" was set in Solvang and the surrounding Santa Ynez Valley.

Because of its location in wine country, Scandinavian ambiance and over 340 days of sunshine, Solvang has become a huge tourist attraction with over one million visitors per year.

Once in the valley, discover the charm of nearby Santa Ynez, Ballard and Los Olivos. Santa Barbara, often referred to as the American Riviera, is roughly 50 miles south of Solvang. For those looking for a day at the beach, the Pacific Ocean is only 20 minutes away.

Solvang was once named one of the "Ten Most Beautiful Small Towns in the Western United States" by *Sunset* magazine. If you ever wanted to visit Denmark without traveling all the way to Europe, make your way to Solvang. Some say it looks more like Denmark than Denmark. And you don't need a passport.

LEFT AND BELOW LEFT: The Solvang Folk Dancers entertain at Danish Days.

BELOW RIGHT: Authentic Danish costumes can be found in the Solvang Children's Shop.

OPPOSITE PAGE CLOCKWISE: The Fresno Danish Dancers, wooden shoes of all sizes and children dressed in Danish outfits add charm to Solvang.

SOLVANG

ABOVE: Elverhøj Museum of History and Art, housed in a historic handcrafted structure, is one of the few museums outside of Denmark devoted to Danish history and the Danish-American spirit. The name Elverhøj comes from Denmark's 1828 folk play "Elverhøj."

LEFT: The 700-seat outdoor Solvang Festival Theater hosts many concerts and events.

INTRODUCTION

ABOVE LEFT: Storks peer down from just about every rooftop in the village. In Denmark, where the European white stork once nested, storks are believed to bring good luck. Unique weathervanes grace many of the roof tops.

ABOVE: A wooden ship hangs from the ceiling inside Bethania Lutheran as a reminder that Denmark is a seafaring nation.

LEFT: Solvang would not be complete without a replica of Copenhagen's Little Mermaid statue. The bronze statue is based on the 1837 fairy tale "The Little Mermaid" by Hans Christian Andersen.

OPPOSITE PAGE CLOCKWISE: Ballard's Little Red Schoolhouse was built in 1883. The first of Solvang's windmills, built by Ferd Sorenson, still stands near the east side of the village. Wrought iron lanterns found throughout the village add an Old World look to Solvang. An ad for Tuborg beer, a Danish brewing company founded in 1873, is tucked out of the way in Hans Christian Andersen Square.

RIGHT: An authentic Danish thatched roof shelters the tasting room, art gallery and gift shop of Lions Peak Vineyards in the heart of the village. A thatched roof is made of small reeds woven tightly together.

BELOW LEFT: The Book Loft is the hometown bookstore. Upstairs you will find The Hans Christian Andersen Museum.

BELOW RIGHT: These little houses, seen all over the village, are a clever disguise for the public address system used during celebrations and other events.

INTRODUCTION

RIGHT: Discover Old World charm at the Wine Valley Inn with its three-story clock tower.

OPPOSITE PAGE CLOCKWISE: Sunny Fields Park, Solvang Elementary School built in 1940, the entrance to Hans Christian Andersen Park and Solvang Park.

BELOW: The River Course at Alisal has breathtaking views of the Santa Ynez Mountains and Valley.

Once upon a time a thousand years ago there was a king of DENMARK named Gorm the Old. All through the years his family has ruled the oldest kingdom of the world, and the present Queen Margrethe the Second is a descendant of the old king Gorm.

ABOVE AND OPPOSITE PAGE LEFT: The artwork on the wall of Birkholm's Bakery features the Danish Royal Family, from Viking Gorm the Old to present Queen Margrethe II.

The Village

With its Danish-inspired architecture, clock towers, windmills and Scandinavian bakeries, Solvang may be more Danish than Denmark. Names like Petersen, Nielsen, Jensen and Rasmussen are common.

The adorable pedestrian-friendly village with fluttering flags is filled with wine-tasting rooms, tempting pastry shops, antique stores, boutiques and gift shops packed with everything from cuckoo clocks to colorful Danish clogs. And shopkeepers dressed in Danish costumes add the finishing touch.

Since the village only covers about ten blocks you should walk it to really enjoy it. Or you may prefer to ride on a horse-drawn trolley or fit the family into a rented four-wheel surrey cycle. There's plenty to do and see as well as eat and taste. The shaded Solvang Park is a good place to have a picnic or just relax.

Solvang is now dubbed the "Danish Capital of America" but the idea of a Danish village didn't take hold until the mid 1940s. Locals such as Ferdinand Sorensen and Earl Petersen were pioneers of the Scandinavian style that gives the town its charming Danish flavor.

At that time, windmills began to sprout up and many of the original buildings were restyled with *bindingsverk* framing (half-timbered), simulated thatched roofs and charming dormers. Main Street was renamed Copenhagen Drive and other streets were given Danish names.

Although Solvang is now a thriving tourist attraction with over a million visitors a year, it still has a friendly small town atmosphere and warm hospitality. *Kom snart igen!* (come back soon!).

SOLVANG

LEFT: The copper-roofed buildings along Alisal Road at sunrise.

BELOW LEFT: Solvang Antique Center and Clock Tower.

BELOW RIGHT: Enjoy Old World hospitality at the tiled-roof and half-timbered Petersen Village Inn.

OPPOSITE PAGE: Images along Mission Drive.

Solvang
SOLVANG NEEDLEWORK
Jule Hus

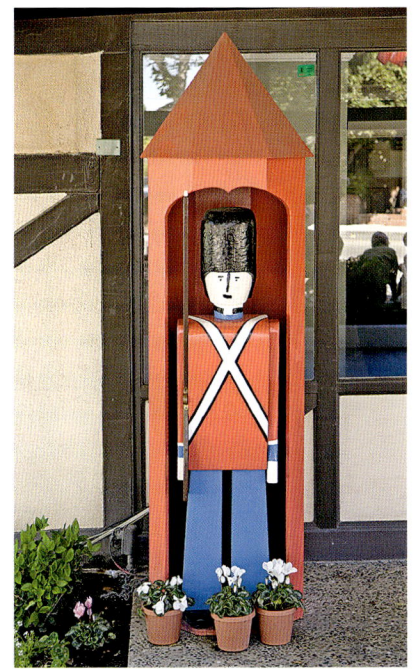

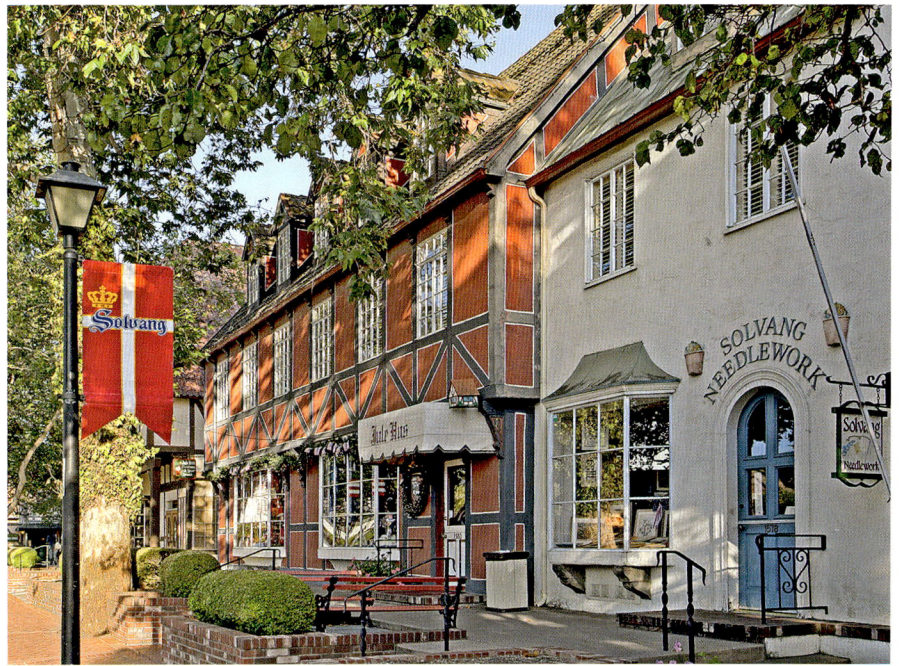

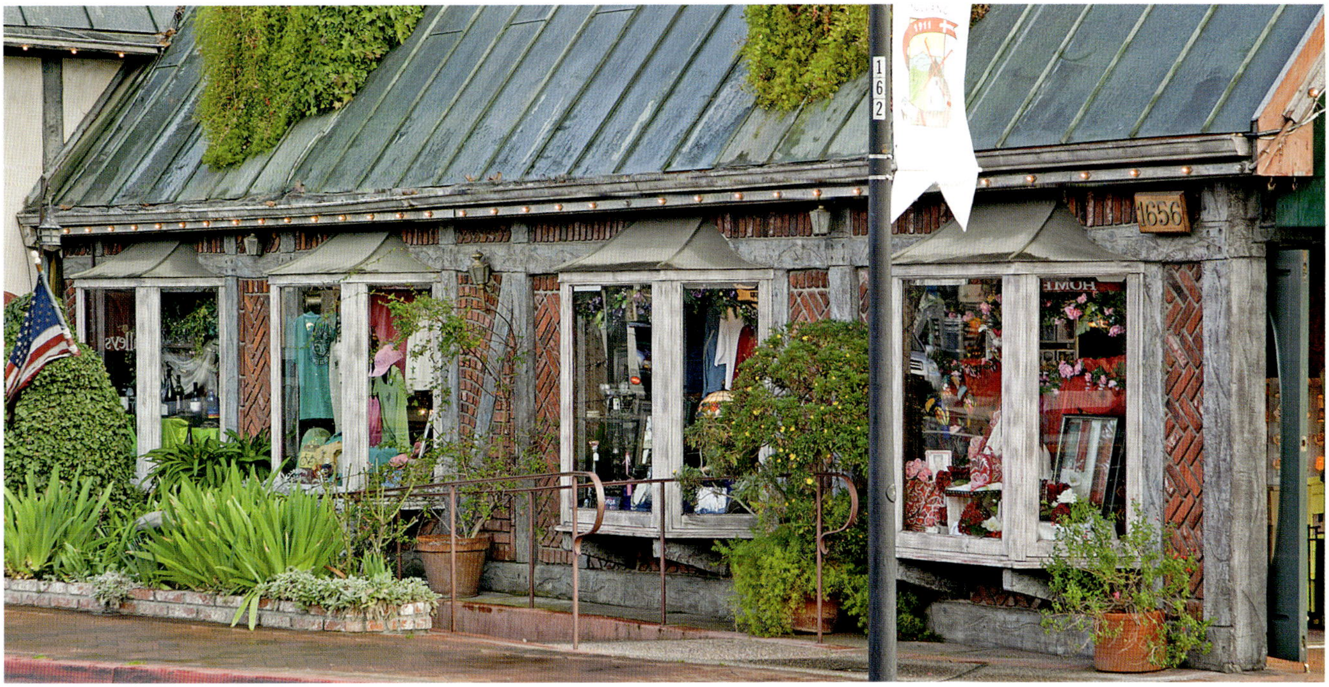
162
1656

RIGHT: From left to right are Del Sole, Hanson's Clock Shop and the Bit O' Denmark restaurant. Built in 1911, the Bit O' Denmark was the home of the original folk school until it moved to Atterdag College in 1914.

OPPOSITE PAGE: The bronze statue of Hans Christian Andersen, the renowned Danish fairy tale writer, was sculpted by Henry Luckow Nielsen of Copenhagen.

BELOW RIGHT: Petersen Village Square is nestled in the heart of Solvang.

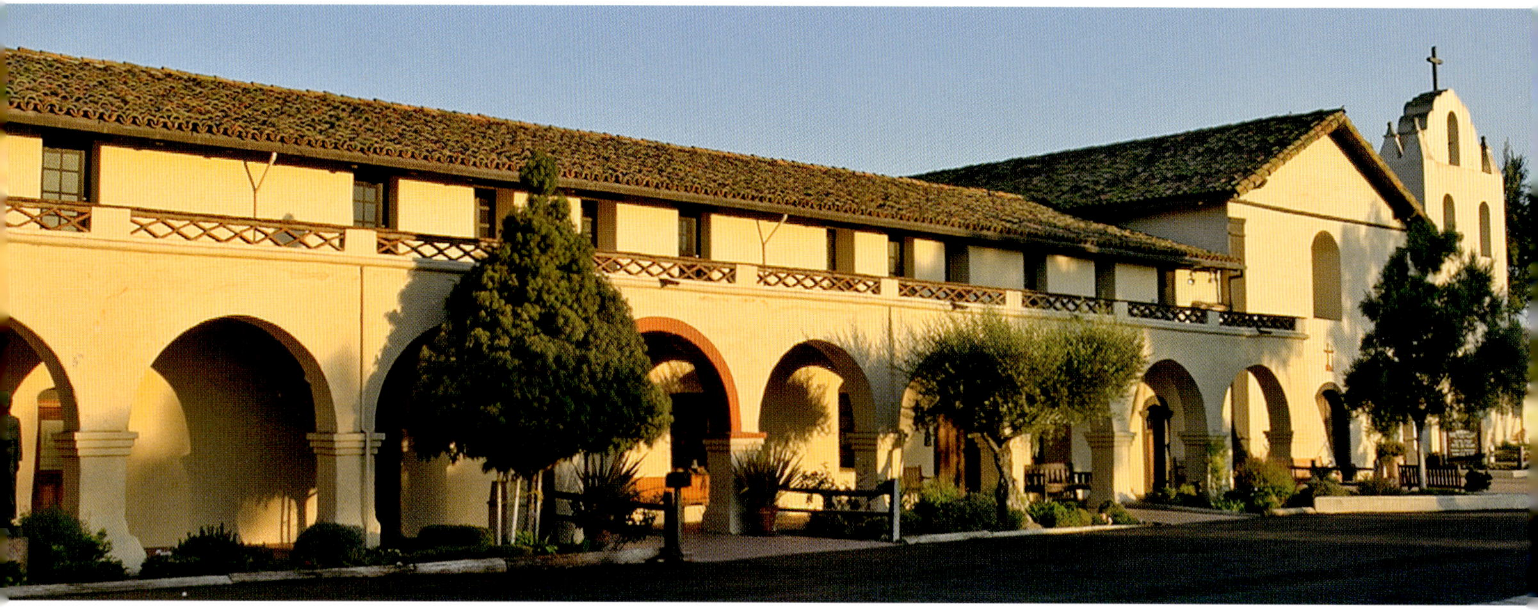

THE VILLAGE

Old Mission Santa Inés, founded in 1804 by Spanish missionaries, is a National Historic Landmark. The classic arch-lined building and bell tower are a treat to explore.

OPPOSITE PAGE: The array of shops, bakeries and cafes has people going in every direction.

RIGHT: Birkholm's Bakery classic delivery truck.

BELOW LEFT: If you want a pair of Danish wooden shoes, look no further. This giant red clog is always in front of the Solvang Shoe Store where Captain the dachshund takes time out to pose. The Jack Russells are patiently waiting their turn.

BELOW RIGHT: Olsen's Danish Village Bakery and Coffee Shop serves baked goods from four generations of family recipes dating back to Denmark in 1890.

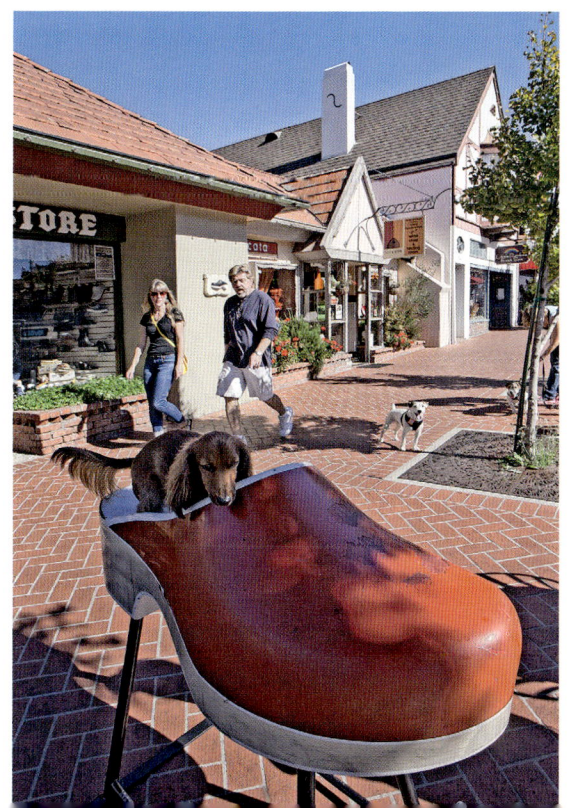

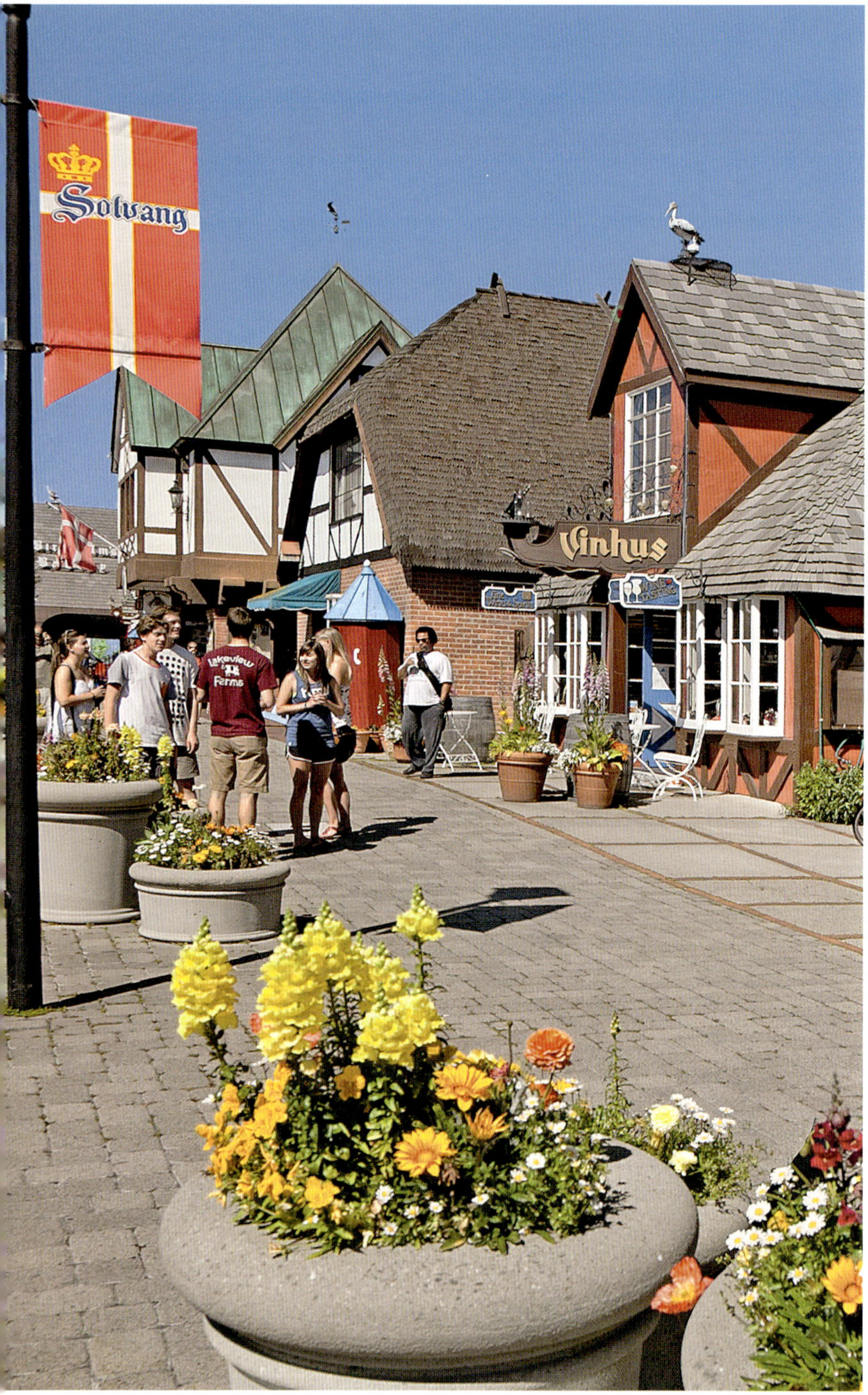
Solvang
Vinhus

SOLVANG INN & COTTAGES

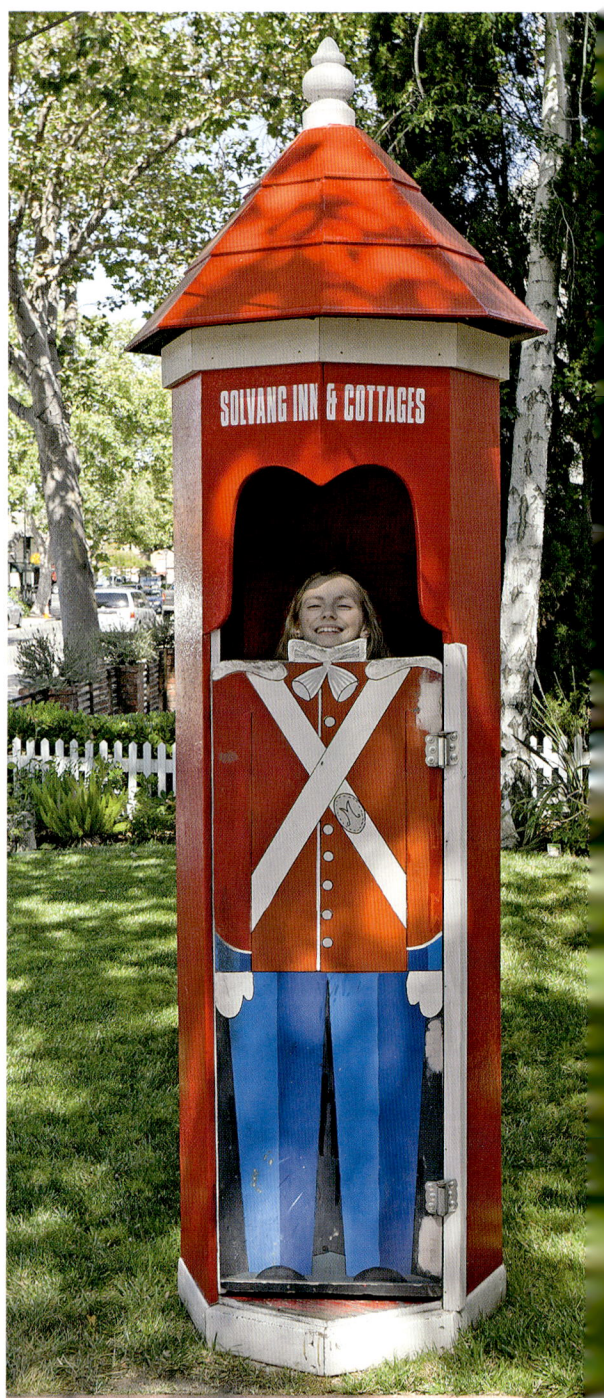

THE VILLAGE

OPPOSITE PAGE LEFT: Colorful Copenhagen Square.

OPPOSITE PAGE RIGHT: A friendly volunteer takes time to pose in one of Solvang Inn and Cottages' guard stations.

RIGHT: Birkholm's Bakery was founded in 1951.

BELOW: Mortensen's Danish Bakery, located in Petersen Village Square, was started by a Danish native and baker from Copenhagen.

If the colorful buildings don't already brighten up the village, an array of vibrant flowers is the icing on the cake.

BELOW LEFT: A bronze statue along Mission Drive.

SOLVANG

THE VILLAGE

The Honen ("The Hen" in Danish), is a Danish-style streetcar pulled by two Belgian horses. The trolley glides around the village as the driver, dressed in a white shirt and red suspenders, entertains the passengers with history and engaging stories.

SOLVANG

ABOVE: Copenhagen Square through Rasmussen's archway on a rainy February evening.

LEFT: Dusk sets in along Alisal Road.

BELOW RIGHT AND PAGE 38 TOP: Night time along Copenhagen Drive.

OPPOSITE PAGE CLOCKWISE: Traci and Lauren's Consignments, Actors Corner and Coffee, Solvang Spinning and Weaving and Family Coats of Arms.

Windmills and Towers

Windmills and towers galore. Solvang's quintet of windmills add a Danish countryside flavor to the village. After returning from Denmark in the 1940s, Ferdinand Sorensen built the town's first windmill alongside his Danish-style home.

Towers of all shapes and sizes jut up through the blue sky. Steep gabled roofs, old-fashioned gas lamps and wrought ironwork add flair and show that details are very important in Solvang.

Bethania Lutheran Church with its corbiestepped gables was designed to look like the rural churches around Denmark. The Round Tower of Solvang, a replica of the one in Copenhagen captures the old country's architecture.

SOLVANG

WINDMILLS AND TOWERS

Built in 1928, Bethania Lutheran was the first building in Solvang with Danish-style architecture.

This was once the home of the Solvang Visitors Center before it was moved to its current location on Copenhagen Drive.

WINDMILLS AND TOWERS

The Clock Tower chimes every hour. Its carillon bells can play 250 songs.

The Round Tower of Solvang is a 1/3-scale replica of the Rundetaarn (Round Tower) in Copenhagen.

Festivals and Celebrations

Festivals and celebrations are traditional ingredients of Solvang's charm and personality.

On Solvang's 25th anniversary in 1936, the village began to celebrate Danish folk traditions during Danish Days. The annual September festival, known for its authentic food, folk dancing, concerts and colorful parades, has helped put Solvang on the map.

Every March since 1993, the Taste of Solvang has featured local foods and wines. Enjoy a walking smorgasbord with delicious bites offered by restaurants and bakeries. Local wineries pour their vintages during the Wine Tasting Room Walks.

Celebrate a European-style Christmas during the annual Julefest. Festivities include a tree lighting ceremony, caroling, a parade and Danish dancing.

Other fun events include the Independence Day Festival and Fireworks and the delightful Old Mission Santa Inés Fiesta in August.

ABOVE: The 2012 Danish Days Maid and a volunteer singer triple the size of Papa Heinz's one-man accordion band.
OPPOSITE PAGE: During Danish Days, the Ravens of Odin re-enactment group sets up an authentic Viking encampment in Solvang Park. The group demonstrates the use of Viking-age weapons.

FESTIVALS AND CELEBRATIONS

The Solvang Village Folk Dancers are a fun and friendly bunch that dances in the streets during Danish Days and performs somewhere in the area all year round. Little Man in a Fix, shown above on the opposite page, is a Danish folk dance with two sets of couples linked arm to arm. If there is an odd number of couples when they switch partners, the couples have to run and find another couple so they will not be in a fix. The women on each end seem to fly through the air.

BELOW LEFT AND OPPOSITE PAGE: The smell of aebleskiver (Danish pastry) and medisterpolse (Danish sausage) fills the air during the Danish Days breakfasts. An assembly line of volunteers dressed in Danish outfits makes sure that nobody goes hungry.

RIGHT: The Solvang Village Band plays from a horse-drawn beer wagon given to Solvang by Denmark's Carlsberg Beer in 1964.

BELOW RIGHT: You can see why aebleskiver is so popular at the Solvang Restaurant. Good thing that you don't have to pronounce it to eat it. The tennis ball-shaped Danish pancake is topped with powdered sugar and raspberry jam.

SOLVANG

FESTIVALS AND CELEBRATIONS

OPPOSITE PAGE: *Tak for Mad* is Danish for "Thanks for Food." Giant Danish pastry balls without the toppings appear to be flung off the gigantic aebleskiver pan and bounce along the street and up into the trees.

RIGHT AND BELOW: The Danish Days parade.

The 90-minute Solvang 4th of July parade.

FESTIVALS AND CELEBRATIONS

63

Doors and Windows

Doors and windows often reveal a great deal about the character of the town.

You will see multi-colored Scandinavian-style doors painted in every color available. Dormers with stained glass windows protrude from many rooftops.

The Old Mission Santa Inés features several arch-topped wooden doors with early-era handles and hinges dating back to 1804.

At night, the storefront windows glow, giving the village a year-round holiday season flair.

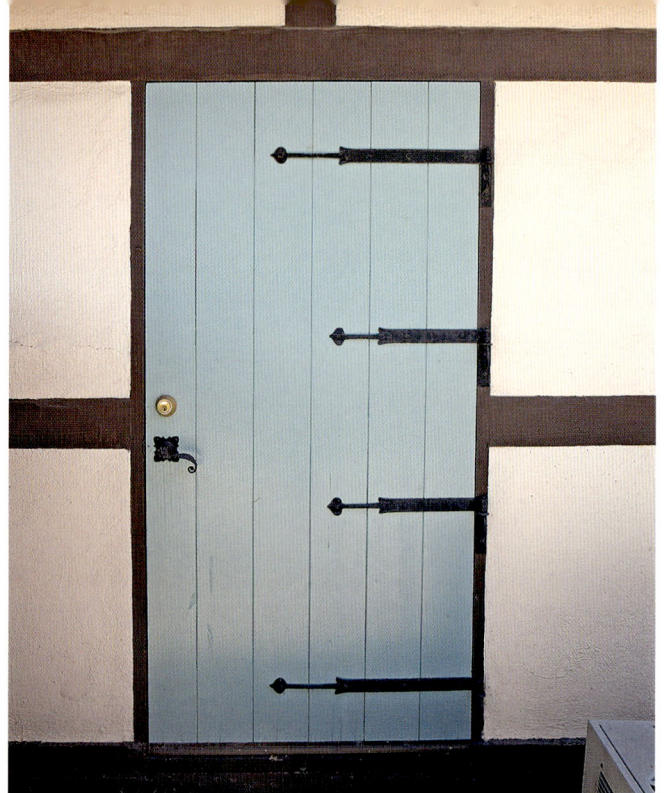

ABOVE: Elverhøj Museum's hand-carved redwood front door with an image of an elfin scene from the Danish folk play "Elverhøj." *Elverhøj* means "elves on a hill."

OPPOSITE PAGE CLOCKWISE: Elverhøj Museum's curvy wrought iron front door hinges, another Elverhøj Museum door, the red door of Solvang Brewing Company and a view inside the Sunstone Winery's stone barrel-aging cave.

SOLVANG

DOORS AND WINDOWS

73

SOLVANG

ABOVE: It's hard to miss the Jule Hus's (Danish for "Christmas House") twinkling red window display, filled with Christmas ornaments, nutcrackers and other European collectables.
The Iron Art Gift Shop (opposite page top) and Edelweiss (opposite page bottom) are among the most eye-catching storefront windows along Copenhagen Drive.

SOLVANG

LEFT: Danish Mill Bakery was founded in Copenhagen and opened in Solvang in 1960 after the family immigrated to the United States.

OPPOSITE PAGE: Elna's Dress Shop has Danish costumes for all ages.

BELOW: Chocolate heaven awaits you at Ingeborg's Danish Chocolate Factory.

Danish Gardens

The gardens and flower-lined sidewalks transform an already colorful village into a kaleidoscopic wonder and add to its Danish character.

As you explore the neighborhoods and charming courtyards you notice that the gardens have a quiet simplicity. You will be tempted to stop and take photos.

PAGE 80, THIS PAGE RIGHT, PAGE 86 LEFT AND PAGE 87 RIGHT: The lush gardens surrounding the quaint Enchanté Cottage Spa.

PAGE 86 BOTTOM RIGHT: Coghlan Vineyard and Jewelers is located in the heart of Los Olivos.

SOLVANG

DANISH GARDENS

A Look Inside

If the aromas from the Danish bakeries and chocolate factories don't invite you in, the shops along the quaint streets overflowing with all kinds of collectables are hard to walk by without stopping in for a look.

If you are looking for a pair of wooden shoes or a Danish costume, you've come to the right place. With over 150 specialty shops in the village, there is something for everyone.

ABOVE: Solvang Restaurant is where you can find Arne's Famous Aebleskiver (inset), as well as other traditional Danish food.
OPPOSITE PAGE TOP: Pearls of Provence. OPPOSITE PAGE BOTTOM: Greda's Iron Art Gift Shop.
PAGE 89: Black Forest chalet clocks fill the walls of the Pebble People Shop.

A LOOK INSIDE

ABOVE: In 1961, a chocolate dipper from one of Denmark's largest chocolate factories opened Ingeborg's Danish Chocolate Factory.

RIGHT: The Rocky Mountain Chocolate Factory.

OPPOSITE PAGE TOP: There are too many choices at Danish Mill Bakery.

OPPOSITE PAGE BOTTOM LEFT: It may be too tempting for some to just peek inside Old Danish Food Farm and Fudge Kitchen.

OPPOSITE PAGE BOTTOM RIGHT: Downey's Dress Shop and Candy World has barrels lined up as far as the eyes can see filled with just about any candy you can imagine.

Around the Valley

Solvang, surrounded by the Santa Ynez and San Rafael Mountain Ranges, is a scenic California treasure not to be missed. Enjoy your favorite wines amidst the vineyards while admiring the ancient oaks covering gently rolling hills.

Most of the Santa Ynez wineries were not established until the 1970s because the area was considered too cold to produce enough grapes for the wines of the day. Experimentation in the 1960s with colder-weather varieties such as Pinot Noir and Chardonnay were quite successful and vineyards quickly began to sprout up. There are now more than 80 to visit.

The valley still has many sprawling ranches and active farms with apple and walnut orchards.

In the spring, poppy fields mixed with lupine carpet the rocky hillsides along Figueroa Mountain.

The rolling countryside makes the valley a popular destination for the elite as well as the casual cyclist.

ABOVE: Wine tasters can relax in Gainey Vineyard's oak-shaded garden.

LEFT: Bunches of purple-colored grapes look poised to be picked in mid November. Grapes thrive in the Santa Ynez Valley's climate of warm days and cool nights.

PAGES 98-99: The Santa Ynez Valley is dotted with ancient oaks stretching over the rolling hills. In the morning, a flow of fog covers the foothills.

ABOVE: The tasting grounds of Sunstone Winery, surrounded by vineyards and views of the foothills, provides the perfect place to relax and enjoy the wines.

RIGHT: Early morning along Alisal Road just outside of Nojoqui Falls County Park.

PAGE 94: When you see California poppies and lupine beginning to bloom along Figueroa Mountain Road, it's a sign that spring has sprung in the Santa Ynez Valley.

SOLVANG

AROUND THE VALLEY

SOLVANG

ABOVE AND OPPOSITE PAGE TOP: Images from around the nearby town of Santa Ynez.
OPPOSITE PAGE BOTTOM RIGHT: Horses run free at Sky High Farms just on the outskirts of Solvang.
OPPOSITE PAGE BOTTOM LEFT: The Flag Is Up Farm's 5/8-mile oval racetrack is roughly halfway between Solvang and Buellton.

Ostrichland is a fun first stop just before you get to Solvang. The birds peer over the fence waiting to be fed.

AROUND THE VALLEY

SOLVANG

LEFT AND BELOW: The Rideau Vineyard tasting room, located inside a historic 1884 two-story adobe home, is surrounded by a rose-strewn garden, green lawns and lookouts over the vineyard.

ABOVE: Lincourt Vineyard's raised verandah overlooks picturesque vineyards and is a wonderful setting to relax and enjoy a bottle of wine. The vineyard was originally a dairy farm and its tasting room is in an old farmhouse, built in 1926 from a Sears Craftsman kit home.

RIGHT: The Lincourt's rustic barrel room once served as a barn for dairy cattle.

PAGES 106 AND 107: Zaca Mesa Winery and Vineyards, located at 1500 feet in Foxen Canyon, has extraordinary views in every direction.

Other Photo Books By Mike Barton

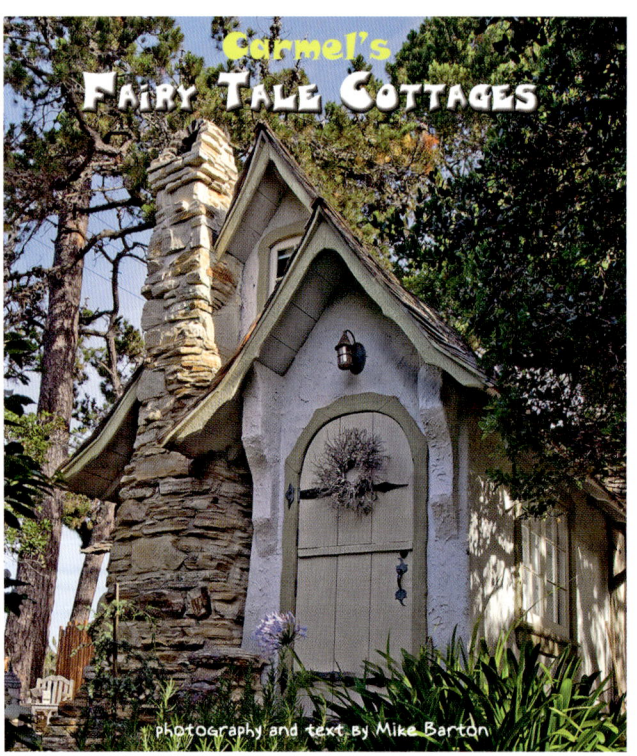

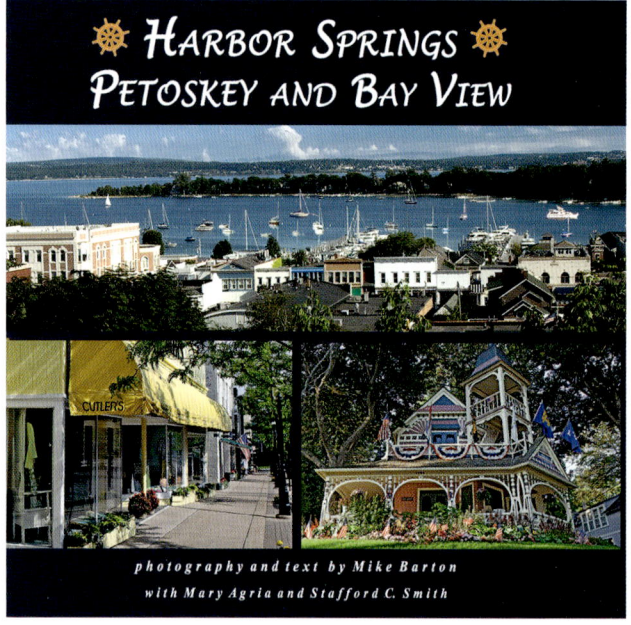

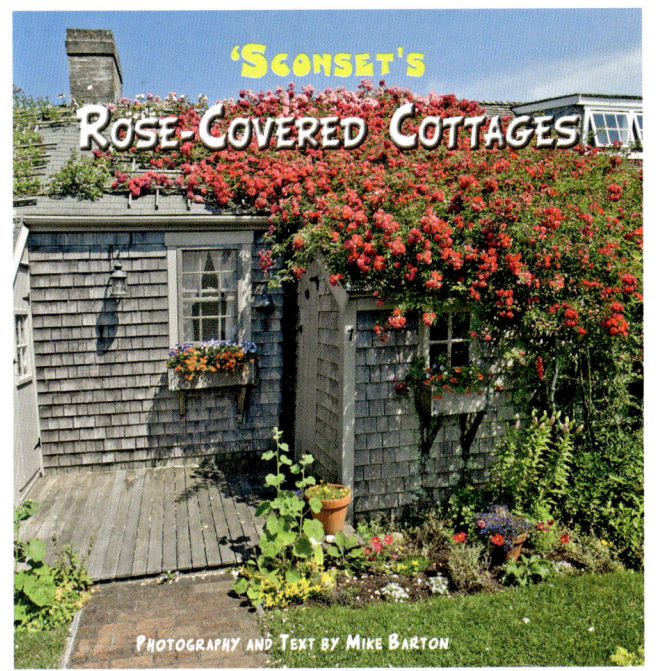

About the Photographer

Mike Barton is a landscape photographer from Solana Beach, California. A native of Michigan, Mike moved to sunny California after graduating from Michigan State and began to photograph the Pacific coast.

Photography became a true passion when he moved to Boulder, Colorado where he tried to photograph every square inch of the Colorado mountains. It was at that time he came up with the idea to make a book on Boulder, his first book.

His next three books were focused on resort towns in Northern Michigan where his parents lived. Then he thought, Why stop there? and kept making books.

Mike began this project on Solvang, his eighth book, when he visited there for the first time in February 2012 after several people suggested it. Since he only lives four hours away, he was able to return five more times during a seven-month period.

Although Mike tries to be at the right place at the right time, he also feels that it is just as important to make the best of it when conditions do not cooperate. A photo can be taken of the same location on different days and the clouds, colors, waves and reflections can vary dramatically.

To see more of Mike's work, please visit his website: www.mikebartonphoto.com.